W9-AJO-048

Legal & Disclaimer

The information contained in this book and its contents is not designed to replace or take the place of any form of medical or professional advice; and is not meant to replace the need for independent medical, financial, legal or other professional advice or services, as may be required. The content and information in this book has been provided for educational and entertainment purposes only.

The content and information contained in this book has been compiled from sources deemed reliable, and it is accurate to the best of the Author's knowledge, information and belief. However, the Author cannot guarantee its accuracy and validity and cannot be held liable for any errors and/or omissions. Further, changes are periodically made to this book as and when needed. Where appropriate and/or necessary, you must consult a professional (including but not limited to your doctor, attorney, financial advisor or such other professional advisor) before using any of the suggested remedies, techniques, or information in this book.

Upon using the contents and information contained in this book, you agree to hold harmless the Author from and against any damages, costs, and expenses, including any legal fees potentially resulting from the application of any of the information provided by this book. This disclaimer applies to any loss, damages or injury caused by the use and application, whether directly or indirectly, of any advice or information presented, whether for breach of contract, tort, negligence, personal injury, criminal intent, or under any other cause of action.

You agree to accept all risks of using the information presented inside this book.

You agree that by continuing to read this book, where appropriate and/or necessary, you shall consult a professional (including but not limited to your doctor, attorney, or financial advisor or such other advisor as needed) before using any of the suggested remedies, techniques, or information in this book.

My Dear readers,

Diabetes is a condition that can be managed well, provided you adhere to the advice provided by your healthcare provider.

All adjustments should be done under expert medical supervision.

After reading this book, in order to change your diet, please consult with your doctor!

Thanks for your understanding,
Lisa Nelson

Table of contents

Introduction

First of all, I thank and congratulate you for downloading this book. You are probably seeking for Diabetes information, and you have come to right place. This book contains the things you need to know regarding this disease.

Before digging deeper, let me introduce to you a detail of history relating to diabetes and some additional facts related to it. This particular disease can be traced way back to ancient Egypt. As a matter of fact, diabetes was one of the first diseases ever described. The proof is an Egyptian manuscript all the way from 1500 BCE that states the words "too great emptying the urine." These first cases are believed to have been the Type 1 diabetes.

The word diabetes originally means "to pass through" or "a passer through" and was first utilized in 230 BCE by the Greek Apollonius. However, in the Roman Empire, this disease is typically rare. This might be due to the kind of lifestyle and diet the people in this age have. Galen who claimed that he had only seen two cases of this his entire life also referred this disease as the "diarrhea of urine."

Thanks for downloading this book. It's my firm belief that it will provide you with all the answers to your questions

Chapter 1: Diabetes Unmasked

What is Diabetes?

Diabetes is a chronic health condition in which your body demonstrates a reduced ability to remove glucose from your blood and into its cells after eating or drinking anything that contains carbohydrates. This reduced ability leads to hyperglycemia or elevated blood glucose level.

It is often referred to as the 'silent killer' because many individuals do not even know that they have it.

Your body uses a variety of enzymes to break down the food that you eat. Food is divided into macro and micro nutrients which in turn are used in different parts of the body for various jobs. As an example, the fat is used to facilitate brain health whereas the carbohydrates are used to provide energy to the body.

The carbohydrates are the complex sugars that are broken down into simpler forms referred to as glucose. Glucose is then released into your blood stream for immediate release as energy or for storage to facilitate later use.

To store and use glucose, your body produces a hormone called insulin. This is manufactured by the beta cells in your pancreas. These cells are sensitive to the concentration of insulin in your bloodstream and can release it on an as-needed basis. They monitor the amount of blood sugar in your blood stream to elevate or decrease the production of insulin. The beta cells in your pancreas need to release more insulin to deal with the elevated blood glucose level.

Now, as this insulin is produced, the enzymes activate other cells in your body telling them to accept glucose as energy. This gradually diminishes the amount of glucose circulating in the bloodstream, leading to decreased production of insulin. The process is a continuous one and is not dependent on what, how and when you eat. Blood sugar level can increase in your bloodstream after consumption of a high carbohydrate diet, even if you do not have diabetes.
The balance between energy and insulin is what provides you the energy to function normally. Diabetes as a disease impacts this process and therefore the ability of your body to naturally produce insulin in balanced amounts.

Depending on the kind of diabetes that you have been impacted with, the natural process can be impacted in some ways this may include the inability of beta cells in your pancreas to produce insulin as a consequence of being over-worked. As your blood glucose level reaches 180 mg/dl, your kidneys attempt to flush out the excess glucose through urination. This is primarily the reason why excessive urination and thirst are vital signs of diabetes.

If unchecked, diabetes can be a serious, even life-threatening disease leading to threatening complications such as blindness, gangrenes or even death due to a diabetic coma. Let us first try and understand the kind of diabetes that you have.

Types and Causes of Diabetes

Type 1 diabetes

In type 1 diabetes, the patient's pancreas manufactures little to no insulin naturally. In fact, they often lack the actual beta cells needed for the production of insulin. In cases where beta cells are being attacked and destroyed, the symptoms only appear when the number of cells goes down.

Most medical practitioners believe that type 1 diabetes is genetic. However, a few attribute this to a viral attack too! Some scientists believe that it is caused by the immune system attacking the pancreas, destroying beta cells and stopping them from functioning.

Others feel that it is your body's reaction to certain viruses that initiates this in error. Scientists, however, agree that there is a genetic predisposition involved.

People with type 1 diabetes will have the disease for life since if the cells that produce insulin are destroyed, they cannot be reproduced.

Patients diagnosed with IDDM (insulin dependent diabetes mellitus) may require regular insulin injections. The symptoms of insulin dependent diabetes may include tiredness, unexplained weight loss, increased need to urinate, general itchiness, and excessive thirst. Often misdiagnosed as type 2 diabetes.

Complications of type 1 diabetes include ketoacidosis and hypoglycemia. It may also lead to conditions such as kidney failure, neuropathy, retinopathy, stroke and heart diseases.

Type 2 diabetes

Type 2 diabetes is also called diabetes mellitus. It frequently impacts overweight individuals, especially during their old age. A sedentary lifestyle has been attributed as the main cause for this kind of diabetes. It is called the adult onset diabetes although some children are also being diagnosed with type 2 diabetes primarily because of their sedentary lifestyles. Around 90% of the total diabetic cases are type 2 diabetic cases.

In this kind of diabetes, the pancreatic cells can produce healthy amounts of insulin. However, for reasons unknown, your body is unable to use this insulin effectively. This condition is also called insulin resistance. The ineffective insulin levels in your body lead to spikes in your blood sugar level, which in turn damages your cells.

Triggered by a sedentary lifestyle, this form of diabetes can be hereditary as well, in case your parent or sibling has ever been diagnosed with diabetes.

Here are a few risk factors for this kind of diabetes:

•Being overweight

- Sedentary lifestyle

- Relatives previously diagnosed with diabetes

- Unhealthy diet

- Smoking

- High blood pressure

- African-Caribbean descent or Asian descent

Type 2 diabetes triggers after 40, the common symptoms including excessive thirst, frequent urination, nausea, blurred vision, weight loss, slow wound healing, along with a loss of muscle mass, tiredness, and hunger. Sometimes these symptoms persist for months, and even diabetics are unable to figure out that they have been impacted.

The chance of inheriting type 2 diabetes in children is as high as 75% in case both parents have been previously diagnosed with diabetes. The onset of type 2 diabetes is not as immediate as type 1 diabetes. In fact, there may be certain individuals who may not demonstrate any visible symptoms.

The treatment involves dietary and lifestyle modifications, incorporating moderate forms of exercise and eliminating unhealthy foods. Sometimes, you may need to take diabetic medications too.

People who have from type 2 diabetes are advised to keep a check on their blood sugar levels to avoid diabetic complications.

Patients have even advised insulin injections in case their condition worsens.

Factors that cause Diabetes

To eliminate diabetes from your life, you must understand the factors that cause it. Here are some of these factors:

Obesity: Being overweight or obese has been identified as the number one risk factor for diabetes. In fact, 80% of people diagnosed with type 2 diabetes are overweight.

Cigarette Smoking: Cigarette smoke elevates the level of inflammation in your body. This increases the risk of diabetes in smokers as opposed to non-smokers.

Smoking can also raise the degree of blood glucose in your body and hence worsen your insulin resistance.

Physical Inactivity: Physical Inactivity can increase your risk of diabetes, even if you are not overweight or obese. On the other hand, in case you are overweight or obese physical activity can help you reduce your risk of diabetes.

Saturated Fats: Replacing your saturated fat with healthy fats such as avocados, nuts and olive oil can reduce insulin resistance.

Low Fiber Diet: A diet rich in fiber helps in decreasing the amount of insulin needed after a snack or meal.

Sugar-Sweetened Beverages: Research shows that people who consume as low as two sugar-sweetened beverages in a day have a 26% higher risk of developing type 2 diabetes than individuals who drink less than one soda a month.

Men with Low Testosterone: Research is now showing that low testosterone and diabetes have a connection and that men with type 2 diabetes are two times more likely to have lower testosterone. Low testosterone can lead to a decrease in libido, erectile dysfunction and lack of energy but the good news is that testosterone can be naturally boosted with some wise choices.

Foods to Avoid

Ideally, diabetics must stay away from any food that leads to a spike in blood sugar level. This includes foods with a glycemic index of 50 or more. Most processed foods will fall into this category since they do not have the necessary fiber needed to balance their carbohydrate content.

Some diets that you must categorically avoid:

Coffee: But coffee has loads of antioxidants? True! Coffee is loaded with so many antioxidants that it is referred to as the health drink. However, the problem with commercial coffee drinks is that they are full of too much sugar and fat. In fact, an actual serving of coffee at Star- bucks is equivalent to five servings!

Now, it is possible to make your very own much friendlier version of coffee. However, a better option is to ditch the coffee completely and opt for tea instead.

Nachos: Corn is a very high sugar vegetable, and nachos chips are created from this vegetable. And as if this is not enough, they are loaded with salt and high in calories owing to their deep fried nature. The high-calorie content of nachos converts a single serving into a full meal!

Juices and juice drink: A number of juices contain added sugar in addition to the high sugar content from the fruit juice itself. The seeds and pulp are filtered out of the juice, leaving no fiber for healthy digestion. In fact, fruit drinks are considered as bad as sugary sodas since they load up a healthy diet with unnecessary sugar. In fact, a single serving of fruit juice is full of 31 gm of carbohydrates.

Rolls and Pastries: The fresh smell of cinnamon, freshly glazed, topped with strawberries and nuts pastries are difficult to resist, aren't they. The high carbohydrate content is a result of 100% white flour loaded with white sugar.

Well, the homemade versions are equally dangerous, even if your try and reduce the serving size to prevent sugar spikes.

Cookies come in the same category, and many cookies are nothing but empty carbohydrate and fats. Home baked cookies can be made healthier using recipes with whole grains and high fiber. However, it must always be remembered that these are also not too great for a diabetic. You may have a home baked cookie occasionally to satisfy your sweet tooth.

Processed meats: You have probably always looked at your roasted turkey as the best food choice ever. It is, however, important to understand that the processed packaged version is full of extra salt and sugar to improve the taste. Try and cut your meat to (or "intending to") improving the taste and reduce the sugar and salt that you are consuming.

Store-bought Smoothies: Juices and smoothies are the latest health fad.

These colorful drinks are however full of sugar and other additives that diminish the power of vitamins in your smoothie. Moreover, the market versions are served in extra-large packing's which are typically five times the size of an actual serving.

While a homemade smoothie can help you meet around 90% of your nutritional requirements, the store-bought versions can run havoc on your health by causing a 200% spike in carbohydrate levels.

Chinese foods: Most Chinese foods are cooked by frying in saturated fat and are loaded with high sugar sauces. The carbohydrate filled white rice is nothing but empty calories. Brown rice is considered as a healthy alternative, however, is still laden with carbohydrates. If you must eat Chinese, try and consume brown rice as the fiber content in brown rice at least attempting to compensate for the carbohydrate content. Also, try and cook your food at home using diabetic friendly sugar-free sauces.

Hamburgers: Those cheese laden burgers that you get at Mc Donald's taste heavenly, but are loaded with carbohydrates, and added sodium, cholesterol, and sugar. Plus, the size of the burger is around four to five times the recommended size which is enough to lead to a major blood sugar spike.

But I love my burgers!

Well, if you must have burgers, try to create your burger at home with freshly ground meat trust me, it is not only going to be much healthier, but also super tastier.

Bread and pizza: The crust of your store bought pizza is loaded with refined flour, excess sugar, unwanted and unhealthy sodium and saturated fats. The meat used is processed using sugar and sodium along with other unhealthy additives. A full pizza can be as high as 900 calories. Top it with a few extras and you know you have exhausted more than half of your calorie requirement for the day!

Pasta and commercial bread are equally dangerous owing to their high glycemic index. Choose a whole wheat option that may temper the carbohydrate content.

However, it will still lead to blood sugar spikes and not fill you up for long.

Managing Your Diabetes

Some individuals mistake their symptoms for some other condition and hence their diabetes remains undiagnosed for a long time.

Hence the first tip to managing diabetes once you become aware that you have been impacted is not to *panic* – Diabetes is a condition that can be managed well, provided you adhere to the advice provided by your healthcare provider.

All that is required from your side is the willingness to educate yourself about your condition, awareness of its complications and readiness to follow a strict dietary and lifestyle protocol. You may also need to take your medicines (whatever your healthcare provider recommends). You will also need to monitor your blood glucose levels at home sometimes these may become dangerously low when you do not eat at regular intervals or when you are using certain herbs along with prescription medication.

Your main focus should be on ensuring that your blood glucose, blood pressure, and cholesterol levels are in control.

Here are some tips to manage your diabetes:

Medications: The first line of action to treat your type 2 diabetes is anti-diabetic drugs and oral or IV insulin administration.

Typically, insulin therapy is prescribed for type 1 diabetes. However, it may be required for particular type 2 cases as well. You must monitor your blood sugar levels closely since type 2 diabetes is a progressive condition and may need you to adjust your medications depending on your blood sugar level. All adjustments should be done under expert medical supervision.

However, there are several other attached conditions other than relying on medicines to control your diabetes, which we will discuss further.

Regular examination of blood glucose levels: If possible, you should monitor your blood glucose levels every day to ensure that everything is under control. Medications, stress, physical activity, other illnesses and the foods you eat can affect your blood glucose levels. Some people avoid regular blood sugar testing. My suggestion is to consult with your health care provider on the frequency at which you will need to check.

Quality Sleep: Quality sleep is vital to manage diabetes effectively. Even only a night of sleep deficiency can reduce your sensitivity to insulin by almost 25%. Reduced sleep or insomnia can result in hormone fluctuations which in turn leads to an elevation in your blood glucose levels.

Stress Management: Physical or mental stress can aggravate your diabetes. The degree at which stress impacts your blood glucose levels varies from one person to another. Studies show that almost all kinds of stress lead to a blood sugar spike. You will read about some incredible stress management techniques.

Quit Smoking: Smoking elevates your risk of diabetes. If you are a smoker, dealing with complications of diabetes becomes all the more difficult. The reason for this is because smoking narrows your blood vessels, elevates your blood glucose levels and leads to inflammations. This also means that there is an increased threat of blood vessel damage, kidney damage, and foot and leg infections in smokers.

Regular Health Checkups: It is important to go for routine check-ups regularly. This ensures that any complication is detected and treated at an early stage itself. Self-evaluation through regular monitoring of blood sugar, blood glucose, weight, and foot evaluation is vitally necessary. Your doctor may advise you to go for regular blood tests, including the A1C test. This is a blood marker that provides average blood sugar data for the past three months.

Alternative forms of treatment: Before beginning with any alternative therapies, it is important to consult with your health care provider. Such treatments options are holistic and impact all parts of a person's life. In some individuals, symptoms of diabetes can be treated with alternative therapies such as:

•Aromatherapy

•Guided Imagery

•Ayurveda

•Homeopathy

•Massage Therapy

•Biofeedback

•Dietary Supplements

•Chinese Medicine and Acupuncture

•Color, Music or Art Therapy

•Herbal and Natural Therapies

Chapter 2: Useful Recipes For Each Day For Diabetics

Breakfast recipes

Orange Salmon

Cooking time: 7 minutes

Ingredients

6 (6-8 ounce) salmon fillets (about 1" thick)

2 teaspoons of garlic powder

1 teaspoon salt

½ teaspoon pepper

1 Orange, cut into sections

3 Tablespoons chopped onion

2 Tablespoons chopped red onion

3 Tablespoons chopped bell pepper

3 Tablespoons lime juice

¼ cup orange juice

Directions

Preheat the oven to 350 degrees.

Season the fish then boil the onions and bell peppers with the juices until tender. Place half onto the fish.

Bake until flaky then flip and add the juices to the other side and bake until flaky and tender but not dry, approximately 5-10 minutes on each side.

Garnish with the orange slices.

Tangy Green Salad

Cooking time: 7 minutes

Ingredients

4 teaspoons white wine vinegar

1/2 cup cherry tomatoes, halved

2 teaspoons olive oil

Dash pepper

1/8- teaspoon salt

2 teaspoons minced fresh basil

3 cups torn mixed salad greens

¾- teaspoon honey

1 tablespoon shredded Parmesan cheese

Directions

Whisk vinegar, fresh basil, olive oil, honey, salt and dash pepper in a small bowl until blended.

In a separate large bowl combine tomatoes and salad greens. Drizzle with vinaigrette and sprinkle with cheese.

Enjoy your meal.

Diabetic Date Dainties

Cooking time: 7 minutes

Ingredients

2 eggs

1 ½- tsp. liquid sweetener

1 ½- tsp. baking powder

1/3 cup dates, chopped

¼- cup flour

½- cup nuts

1 ½- cup bread crumbs

Directions

Beat eggs, sweetener and baking powder.

Add dates, flour and nuts. Stir in bread crumbs.

Chill, then measure by teaspoon on a greased cookie sheet.

Bake at 375 degrees for 12 minutes

Sugar - Free Cranberry Relish

Cooking time: 7 minutes

Ingredients

2 cup cranberries

2 apples

1 cup orange juice

Directions

Grind together the cranberries and apples, using a sweet apple (May also use a blender).

Add orange juice, chopped nuts and sweetener to taste.

Refrigerate several hours before using.

Banana-Spiced Oatmeal

Cooking time: 7 minutes

Ingredients

3 cups water

1 ½- cups quick-cooking oats

2 ripe medium bananas, peeled and diced

3 tablespoons pourable sugar substitute

2 teaspoons ground cinnamon

¼- teaspoon ground nutmeg

1/8 teaspoon salt

1 ½- tablespoons reduced-fat margarine

1 tablespoon vanilla extract

Directions

Bring water to a boil in a large saucepan.

Stir in the oats, return just to a boil, reduce heat and simmer, uncovered, 1 minute.

Remove from heat; add remaining ingredients, cover, and let stand 5 minutes to absorb flavors.

Lunch recipes

Roasted Cauliflower

Cooking time: 7 minutes

Ingredients

8 cups bite-size cauliflower florets

2 tips fresh thyme leaves, roughly chopped

4 cloves medium garlic, chopped

½- cup extra-virgin olive oil

¼- tsp red pepper, crushed

2 tips kosher salt

Directions

Preheat oven to 204°c

Toss cauliflower with red pepper, garlic and olive oil on a baking sheet.

Drizzle salt thyme and salt and then toss again.

Serve on a bowl and enjoy your meal!

Green Beans with Garlic and Lemon

Cooking time: 7 minutes

Ingredients

3 pounds green beans, ends trimmed

1 tbsp. extra-virgin olive oil

2 tbsps. butter

2 medium minced garlic cloves,

1 tsp red pepper flakes

1 tbsp. lemon zest

¼-tsp salt

¼-freshly ground black pepper

Directions

In a stock pot with boiling water with salt, blanch green beans until tender and green in color, for about 2-3 minutes. Drain the water and put in a bowl of ice water.

Heat butter and oil over medium heat in a heavy skillet.

Add red pepper flakes and garlic and sauté for about 30-40 seconds.

Add in beans and sauté until they are coated with butter.

Add lemon zest then add pepper and salt to taste.

Enjoy your meal.

Island Chicken Delight

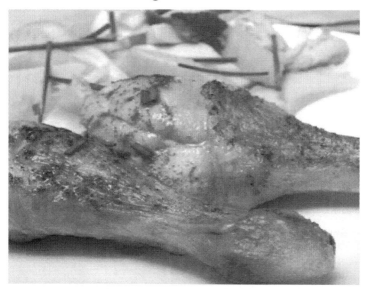

Cooking time: 50 minutes

Ingredients

6-8 (6 ounce) chicken breasts

Salt and pepper to taste'

3 teaspoons garlic powder

¼ cup of orange juice

3 Tablespoons of pineapple juice

Directions

Preheat the oven to 350 degrees.

Season the chicken and then dribble the juices onto the top side.

Lay the pineapple slices on the top as well.

Bake at 350° for 30-45 minute or until done.

Chicken in the Pot

Cooking time: 40 minutes

Ingredients

8-10 chicken wings or drumsticks

1 (14.5 ounce can of stewed tomatoes)

1 cup of fresh okra (or frozen)

½ teaspoon of thyme (powdered)

½ Tablespoon of salt

1 teaspoon of pepper

1 teaspoon of garlic powder

4 dashes of hot sauce

2-2 ½ cups of hot cooked whole grain noodles or spinach noodles

Directions

Brown chicken in a non-stick skillet.

Add remaining ingredients except for the noodles.

Bring to a boil and reduce heat slightly.

Let cook for 30 minutes or until done.

Pour over noodles.

Crock Pot Turkey Tortellini

Cooking time: 5 hours

Ingredients

4 cups chicken or turkey broth

4 cups of water

4 cups of diced tomatoes

2 Tablespoons Italian seasoning

1.9 package of cheese Tortellini (refrigerated)

2 cups fresh spinach

½ cup of Parmesan cheese

Directions

Place broth, water, turkey, tomatoes and seasoning in a 5-quart crock pot.

Cover and cook on lowest setting for about 8 hours or on high for 3-4 hours.

Turn to the highest setting for the last 30 minutes and add Tortellini until tender and then, stir in spinach and cheese.

Dinner recipes

Roasted Cheesy Asparagus

Cooking time: 30 minutes

Ingredients:

1 bunch asparagus

3 tablespoon butter, melted

¾ cup shredded mozzarella cheese

1 tablespoon grated parmesan cheese

Italian seasoning

½-tablespoon house seasoning (garlic powder, pepper and onion powder combined)

Preparation:

Preheat an oven to 425 degrees F (220 degrees C

Line baking sheet, place asparagus on it and sprinkle with melted butter.

Drizzle cheese and seasoning on top.

Put in oven and bake for 15-20 minutes.

Remove and cover the top with mozzarella cheese.

Return into the oven for 4-6 minutes more to melt cheese.

Leave to cool.

Enjoy your meal.

Roasted Carrots

Cooking time: 35 minutes

Ingredients

10 carrots

½- tsp black pepper, freshly ground

3 tbsps. Olive oil

2 tbsps. Fresh dill, minced

1 ¼- tsps. Kosher salt

Directions

Preheat oven to 204°c

Cut the carrots lengthwise if they are thick.

Slice them diagonally into 1-inch-thick size and toss them in a bowl with pepper, salt and olive oil.

Relocate them to a sheet pan and roast for 20-25 minutes in the oven, or until tender and browned.

Toss with minced dill and serve.

Enjoy your meal.

Tuna Boats

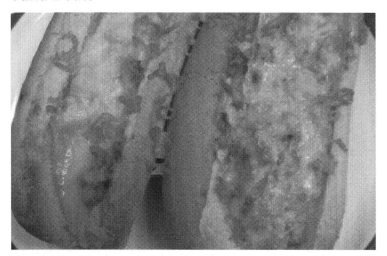

Cooking time: 30 minutes

Ingredients

6 avocados, peeled and sliced

1 large can of tuna fish in water

Several drops of lemon juice

1 teaspoon mayonnaise

1 package of cheddar/Colby cheese

Directions

Mix the tuna, lemon and mayonnaise then dot each avocado half with some of it, sprinkle on cheese and place on a baking sheet in a 350 degree oven until lightly browned.

Veal Appeal with Mushroom

Cooking time: 25 minutes

Ingredients

2 veal chops

6 Tablespoons olive oil, divided

¾ Tablespoons butter

1 Portobello mushroom, chopped

1 ½ cups chicken broth

½ cup of red wine

1 teaspoon fresh rosemary, chopped

Directions

Heat 5 Tablespoons of the oil with butter over a medium heat in a skillet.

Cook the chops in the oil until brown.

Stir in mushrooms, chicken broth, and rosemary and cover while simmering for about 8-10 minutes.

Stir in wine then raise the heat.

Cook until half of the wine is evaporated, removing the chops if they seem to be done so they do not overcook.

Return chops to the pan for one last minute.

Rice and Venison

Cooking time: 20 minutes

Ingredients

1 pound of venison, cubed

1 ½ teaspoons of coconut or olive oil

½ green bell pepper, cut into strips

½ red bell pepper, cut into strips

1 chopped onion

1 (6.8 ounce) package beef flavored rice

Directions

Heat the oil over a medium heat in a skillet and add the venison cubes and cook until browned.

Prepare the rice according to the directions on the package and add the peppers, venison and onion.

Simmer until both the peppers and rice are tender.

Chapter 3: Drinks & desserts for diabetics

Healthy juice

Melon Smoothie

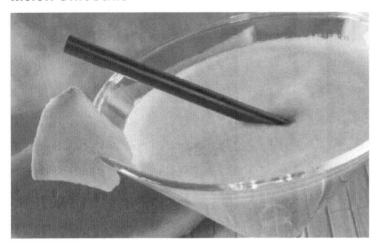

Cooking time: 5 minutes

Ingredients:

1 cup watermelon, seeded and chopped

Juice of 3 limes.

1 cup ice cubes

Preparation:

Put all the ingredients in a blender and blend on high until smooth.

Serve in glasses.

Enjoy your drink.

Apple Burst Smoothie

Cooking time: 5 minutes

Ingredients:

1 green apple

1 cup frozen blueberries

¼ cup apple sauce

½ cup almond milk

1 tbsp. rolled oats

Juice of 1 lemon

Preparation:

Put all the ingredients in a blender and blend on high until smooth.

Serve in glasses.

Enjoy your drink.

Spinach And Kale Green Juice Recipe

Cooking time: 7 minutes

Ingredients:

2 apples, Golden delicious

1 cucumber with peel

1 scant handful of parsley

2 kale stalks

1 lemon (or substitute with 1-2 limes, depending on size)

1 large handful of spinach

Preparation

Wash the kale stalks, parsley and spinach and allow draining.

Next, peel lemon.

Wash cucumber and apples, since you will be leaving the peelings on here.

Once ingredients are prepared, add apples, cucumber, parsley, kale, lemon and spinach to the juicer.

Process until juice is finished.

Drink the juice immediately to get the most from the nutrients.

Enjoy your drink.

Energizing Green Juice Recipe

Cooking time: 7 minutes

Ingredients:

½ cup of kale

1 inch piece of ginger

2 apples

¼ bunch of celery stalks, complete with leaves

¼ head of romaine lettuce

½ of lemon, peeled

½ cup of spinach leaves

¼ fennel bulb

½ of a cucumber

Directions:

Wash kale, celery, romaine and spinach.

Allow the leaves to dry well before you start juicing them.

Wash the rest of the fruits and veggies.

Add the kale, ginger, and apples, celery stalks with leaves, romaine, lemon, spinach leaves, fennel and cucumber to your juice and begin juicing.

Pour your juice into a nice glass.

Enjoy your drink.

Veggie Relaxed Juice Recipe

Cooking time: 6 minutes

Ingredients:

2 carrots

1 cup baby lettuce

1 cup Swiss chard

2 celery sticks

2 branches broccoli

1 teaspoon raw honey

Directions:

Wash and rinse vegetables. Drop carrots into the juicer.

Roll lettuce and Swiss chard leave before running them

through the juicer.

Add celery sticks and broccoli.

Add a teaspoon of honey to sweeten the juice. Enjoy right away.

Non-alcoholic drinks

Veggie Dip

Cooking time: 6 minutes

Ingredients

½ cup plain yogurt

2 tbsps. Pimento, chopped

5 radishes, chopped finely

1 tsp horseradish

2 tbsps. Parsley, chopped

2 tbsps. Scallions, chopped

2 medium carrots, shredded

1 ½- cup low-fat cottage cheese

¼- tsp vegetable salt

Directions

Mash cottage cheese using a fork.

Put in the all the ingredients in a blender and blend until smooth.

Chill before serving.

Enjoy!

Carrot-Apple Power Cocktail

Cooking time: 6 minutes

Ingredients:

6 carrots (organic if possible)

2 apples (organic if possible)

Directions:

Peel the apples and carrots.

Next cut and chop them up.

Put them into your favorite juicer or blender or a combination of juicer/blender and strictly follow the directions of the manual that comes with your machine.

You can always add some raw honey or sweetener depending on your goal with these juices.

If the juice is too strong for you, you might also add some ice cubes or source water.

Enjoy your drink.

Leafy Green Superfood

Cooking time: 7 minutes

Ingredients:

6 leave Kale (organic if possible)

2 cups Spinach (organic if possible)

2 Cucumbers (organic if possible)

4 stalks Celery (organic if possible)

2 apples (organic if possible)

1" ginger root (organic if possible)

Directions:

Peel the cucumbers, apples and ginger.

Cut and chop the fruits and veggies.

Put all the fruits and veggies from the ingredients list into your favorite juicer or blender.

Juice and Blend all the ingredients from the list above together as per instructions.

You can always add some raw honey or sweetener depending on your goal with these juices.

If the juice is too strong for you, you might also add some ice cubes or source water.

Enjoy your drink.

Kale And Cucumber Green Juice

Cooking time: 5 minutes

Ingredients:

4 stalks of celery

1 piece of ginger

6 leaves of kale

½ lemon, peeled

1 cucumber

2 green apples

Preparation:

Before juicing, wash all of the produce thoroughly.

Cut up celery, cucumber and green apples into small enough

pieces to fit into your juicer.

Add all ingredients to your juicer, juicing until complete.

Drink juice immediately.

Add a bit of ice if you like the juice cold.

Enjoy your drink.

Apple And Carrot Juice Recipe

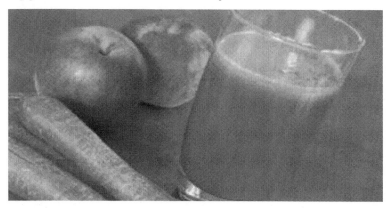

Cooking time: 7 minutes

Ingredients

1 green apple, unpeeled

3-4 large carrots, unpeeled

1 lime, rind removed

½ head of Romaine lettuce

½ bunch of carrot top

3-4 large kale leaves

Preparation:

Start by washing and then coring the apple but leave the peeling on the Apple, since it offers a lot of great nutrients.

Wash the carrots, leaving them unpeeled as well.

Remove the lime rind. In a colander, wash the romaine lettuce leaves, carrot top, and kale leaves thoroughly.

Allow to drain and dry.

Cut carrots and apples into chunks small enough to fit into the juicer.

In a juicer, place the apple, carrots, lime, romaine lettuce, carrot top and kale leaves and then begin juicing.

Pour juice into a nice glass and enjoy quickly getting the most antioxidants and other nutrients.

Enjoy your drink.

Light desserts

Lemony Zucchini Crisp

Cooking time: 30 minutes

Ingredients:

2 medium zucchini, sliced 1/4 inch thick

1-tablespoon lemon zest

½-cup flour

½-cup mayonnaise

2 eggs, lightly beaten

2 cups panko breadcrumbs

Salt and pepper

Preparation:

Preheat oven to 220°C.Scour zucchini slices in flour, dip in egg
and coat with breadcrumb, salt, pepper and lemon zest.
Place zucchini slices on wire rack on a baking pan. Sprinkle oil
lightly and bake in oven for 20-25 minutes.
Puree mayonnaise and serve with zucchini.

Enjoy your meal

Pumpkin Pudding

Cooking time: 35-40 minutes

Ingredients:

2 cups pumpkin puree

½-cup all-purpose flour

¼-cup butter, melted

½-teaspoon salt

1-cup evaporated milk

2 eggs, beaten

1-cup white sugar

2 tablespoons ground cinnamon

½ cup white sugar

1-tablespoon vanilla extract

1 pinch baking soda

Preparation:

Preheat oven to 450°F.

Pour butter in a baking dish.

Whisk 1 cup sugar, evaporated milk, eggs, pumpkin, vanilla extract, baking soda and salt in a large bowl then pour into the baking dish.

Mix cinnamon and remaining ½-cup sugar in a medium bowl and sprinkle on pumpkin mixture.

Bake in the oven for 30-40 minutes and chill to cool.

Enjoy your meal.

Berry And Almond Clafoutis

Cooking time: 30-40 minutes

Ingredients:

¼-cup ground almonds

1 cup frozen raspberries

½-cup castor sugar

1-cup milk

1-punnet blueberries

2 tablespoon butter, chopped

2 large eggs

2-tablespoon plain flour

Preparation:

Preheat oven to 200°C

Butter 4 shallow ovenproof dishes and divide raspberries and blueberries on the dishes.

Whisk together eggs and milk until combined well, then whisk in flour, almonds and 1/3 cup of sugar.

Pour batter on berries, dot with butter and drizzle with sugar remaining.

Bake for 30-40 minutes and leave to cool.

Enjoy your meal.

Cucumber Celery Juice

Cooking time: 5 minutes

Ingredients:

2 large cucumbers

3 large stalk of celery

Preparation:

Wash all the vegetables thoroughly.

Juice each vegetable in this order: cucumbers, Celery.

Stir mixture well before serving.

Enjoy your drink.

Raspberry Soufflé

Cooking time: 35 minutes

Ingredients:

1 tablespoon unsalted butter plus more for greasing

4 eggs, separated

¾ cup granulated sugar plus more for dusting mold

1 pint pureed raspberries

Pinch cream of tartar

Powdered sugar, for dusting

Preparation:

Preheat the oven to 350°F
Grease a soufflé dish with softened butter and coat with

granulated sugar.

Heat ¾-cup sugar, raspberry puree, and butter in a saucepan,

heat over medium heat and cook for 10 minutes.

Remove from heat, remove raspberry seeds and whisk the egg yolks in, one at a time.

Beat egg whites and tartar cream in a separate bowl to soft peaks.

Fold ¼ of the egg whites into raspberry mixture to lighten it then fold the remaining.

Spoon into soufflé dish, put on a cookie sheet and bake for 20-25 minutes on the middle rack.

Dust with powdered sugar.

Enjoy your meal.

Conclusion

I hope this book helped you to learn more about blood sugar and why it is critical to keep it low to maintain or prevent Diabetes. But it's not enough just to know that you should, this book teaches you how to do so and best foods that will assist you in your endeavor.

Whether you essentially have Diabetes, Prediabetes, Low Blood Sugar or Insulin Resistance, keeping your blood sugar balanced and low is imperative. I hope that you now have a better understanding of how it all works and the control that you have to keep your sugar levels healthy.

Not only did you learn what foods are good for lowering your blood sugar, you learned what it is about each and every one that makes it so healthy for those with glucose issues. I hope that helped you with your new lifestyle change, eating to lower your blood sugar on a regular basis.

Just as bad habits develop over the course of time, so do good ones. As you incorporate the knowledge of the things in this book into your daily diet, eating to lower your blood sugar will become a habit, a good habit. And good habits are as hard to break as bad ones are.

Now that you have learned all about how foods affect your blood sugar and have found out which ones help you to lower your blood sugar, it's time to put it into action so you can keep your health high and your blood sugar low.

Thank you and good luck!

My Dear readers,

Diabetes is a condition that can be managed well, provided you adhere to the advice provided by your healthcare provider.

All adjustments should be done under expert medical supervision.

After reading this book, in order to change your diet, please consult with your doctor!

Thanks for your understanding,
Lisa Nelson

Made in the USA
Middletown, DE
14 January 2017